CEREMONY OF CANDLES

A Cantata for Advent and Christmas

by Joseph M. Martin
with Narration by Pamela Martin
Orchestrated by Brant Adams

CONTENTS

Harold Flammer
MUSIC
A Division of Shawnee Press, Inc.

visit Shawnee Press, Inc. online at
www.shawneepress.com

FOREWORD

"Let there be Light," and the shadows of a lowly stable felt the warmth of a new star…

"Let there be Light," and simple shepherds woke to angel glow and brilliant beams of glory...

"Let there be Light," and seeker kings gratefully knelt in manger dust to warm their hearts at the embers of a holy fire...

The Light of the world had come and the people who had walked in darkness began to see the glory of the Lord revealed in the shining eyes of a child named Jesus. Soon his Light would pour from a Bethlehem cave and disperse the shadows of illness, hatred and sin. It would burn in the hearts of faithful followers and reflect in the lives of all those who looked upon his brilliant countenance. Even the darkness of death would surrender as Christ Light burst from a sealed tomb in a thousand beams of radiant life bathing the world in glorious grace.

And now from this one perfect Flame we light our candles of hope and carry them into the shadows of our own time. With carols of faith burning in our souls, we sing the ancient star songs, we share the everlasting story, and with blazing joy we declare to the darkness once again, "Let there be Light."

Joseph M. Martin

PERFORMANCE NOTES

With the motif of Christ coming into the world as Light, begin this cantata with a dimly lit sanctuary. Light a candle at the close of each narration, gradually bringing more and more light to the service, and culminate with a "passing of the light" to the congregation, flooding the sanctuary with the light we are to symbolically carry with us into the world.

If you prefer to end this work by "passing the light" give a small, unlit candle to each choir member and each person who enters the sanctuary. You will also need a Christ candle and nine other candles for the various participants who will place them in designated locations. (Pillar candles would be ideal for altars, communion tables, etc. and tapers placed in candleholders or candelabra would work well elsewhere.)

During the "Procession of Light," the choir processes into the sanctuary led by a choir member carrying a lighted candle. During "In the Bleak Midwinter" the soloist for that piece could bring the lighted candle while singing.

One option is to have this same individual "give" the light to a different person at the close of each narrative. With this option each person will come forward during the narrative to receive the light, the soloist using his/her candle to light each of the others. This would require the soloist to be seated at the front of the sanctuary until the instrumental underscore of "All Is Calm, All Is Bright."

Another option is to have different people either bring in a lighted candle at the end of each narrative, or bring an unlit candle, light it from the candle used for the previous narration and then place it in its receptacle.

The person designated for the narration preceding "In Silence He Came" should bring the Christ candle. If using the option to "pass the light," during the instrumental underscore of "All Is Calm, All Is Bright" the choir may process out of the loft and surround the sanctuary. The soloist for "In the Bleak Midwinter" would then light a small candle (like the ones given to the choir) from the Christ candle, and "pass the light" by lighting the candle of the nearest choir member. This passing of light would continue to each choir member, with choir members standing nearest the end of each pew lighting the candle of the person at the end of that pew so that the light may be passed to the congregation. Then, the narration for "A Blessing of Light" would be read, the anthem sung, and the service dismissed.

If preferred, light only the choir's candles and have the choir members surround the congregation with light. Or, omit the "passing of light" entirely and simply light the final large candle, and have the choir sing "A Blessing of Light" from the loft. Choose what works best in your situation.

Ceremony of Carols
Procession of Lights

Tune: CRANHAM
GUSTAV HOLST (1874-1934)
Arranged by
JOSEPH M. MARTIN (BMI)

ACCOMP.

17

repeat as necessary

NARRATOR: In the day of my favor,

I will say to those in darkness, "Be free!" And the rising sun will come to them from heaven to guide their feet in the path of peace. The wolf will lie down with the lamb and a little child will lead them.

attacca

A8530

In the Bleak Midwinter

Words by
CHRISTINA ROSSETTI (1830-1894), *alt.*

Scottish Folk Tune
Incorporating Tune: **CRANHAM**
GUSTAV HOLST (1874-1934)
Arranged by
JOSEPH M. MARTIN (BMI)

SOPRANO *and* ALTO (*opt. solo*)

In the bleak mid - win - ter, frost - y wind made moan._____ Earth stood hard as

A8530

* Altos sing cued notes when sung by section.

Our God, heav'n can - not hold Him nor earth sus - tain._____ Heav'n and earth shall

might - y,_____ Je - sus Christ!

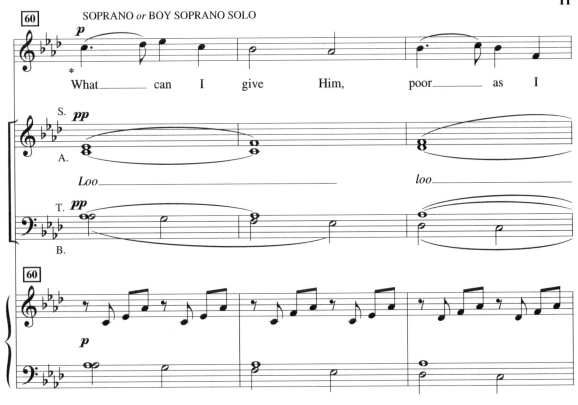

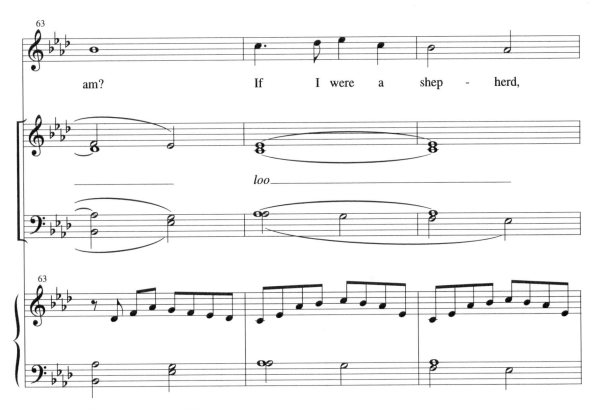

* Tune: CRANHAM, Gustav Holst (1874-1934)

A8530

What___ can I give Him? Give___

What can I give___ Him?___ *Loo*

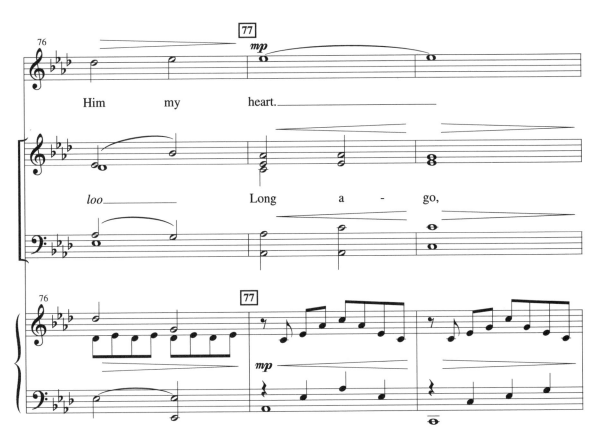

Him my heart._____

*loo*_____ Long a - go,

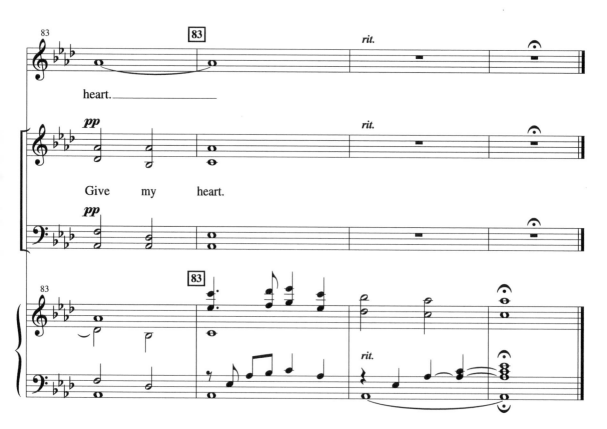

(This page was intentionally left blank.)

NARRATOR:

It came to pass that the people cried out, "We look for light, but darkness surrounds us and we walk in deep shadows." When God heard their cry, he sent the prophet Isaiah with this promise: "In the day of salvation, I will help you. The people walking in darkness will see a great Light; and on those living in the shadows, morning will dawn. I promise to do these things, for I will not forsake you."

The Promised Light

Words by
JOSEPH M. MARTIN

Tune: GOD REST YE MERRY, GENTLEMEN
Traditional English Carol
Arranged by
JOSEPH M. MARTIN (BMI)

A8530

18

A8530

20

A8530

* Tune: VENI EMMANUEL, 15th century Plainsong
Words: anonymous, translation by John M. Neale (1818-1866)

A8530

shall come to Thee, O Is - ra - el.

Now

sing as one and share what

God has done._____ For

God will send a Morn - ing -

NARRATOR:

Let those who walk in darkness, who have no light, trust in the name of the Lord. Believe, for those who place their hope in him will not be disappointed. Wait quietly for the Light of his salvation, for when he comes, darkness will turn to morning, and sorrow to joy.

*to the Glory of God and in celebration of Claudia Place, Organist/Music Director,
on the occasion of her 20th Anniversary of music ministry with
Calvary United Methodist Church, Latham, NY (2004)*

An Advent Credo

Words and Music by
JOSEPH M. MARTIN (BMI)
Flute Arrangement by
JOSEPH M. MARTIN *and*
BRANT ADAMS

* Flute may be played when performed with keyboard. Part is on pages 124-125.
** Tune: CRANHAM, Gustav Holst (1874-1934)

wipe our tears a - way. I be - lieve in

hope. I be - lieve in the life ev - er - last - ing.

mp unis.

I be - lieve in hope. I be - lieve in life ev - er - last - ing.

I be-lieve that Christ will come and bring a bright new

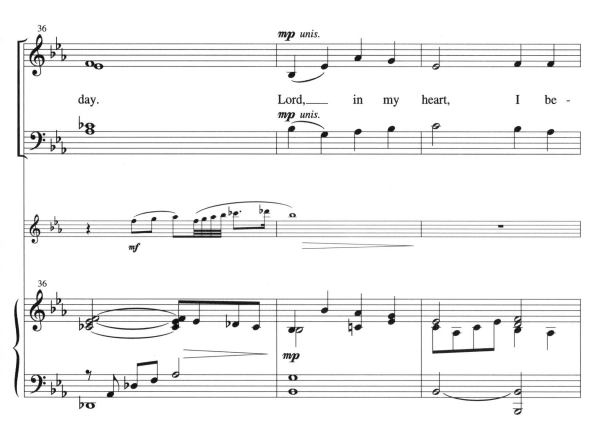

day. Lord, in my heart, I be-

lieve.

When the dark - ness

falls a - round me,   in the still   of the night,

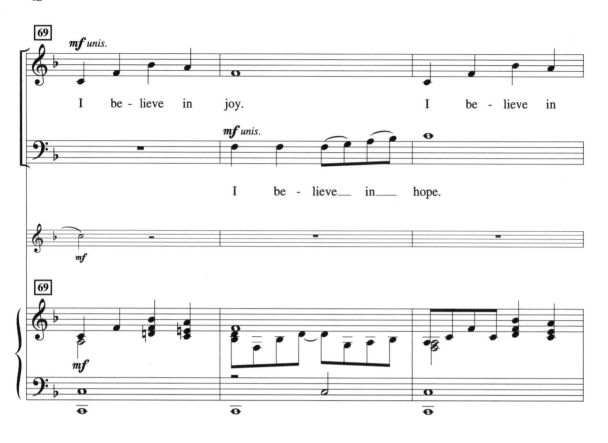

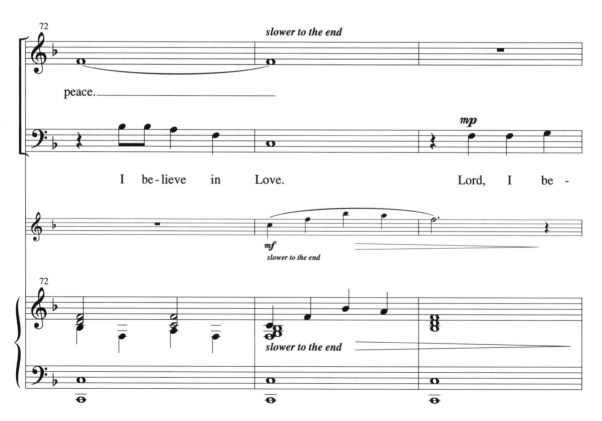

Lord, I be - lieve.

lieve.

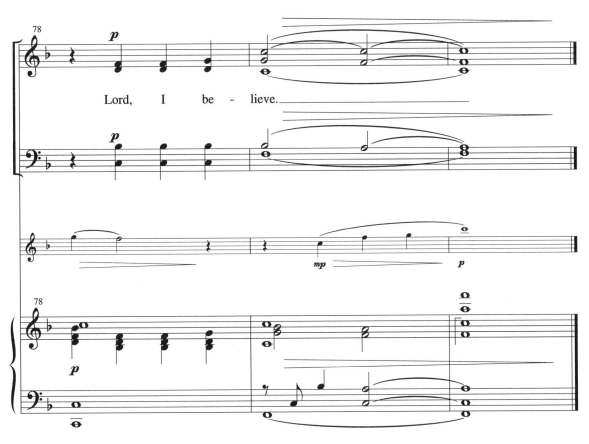

Lord, I be - lieve.

NARRATOR:
Now it was written that the Lord would send a messenger to bear witness to the coming Light. That witness was named John. Hear his voice calling, "Prepare the way for the Lord, for the one true Light. In him is life and that life will be a light for all."

Advent Celebration

Words and Music by
JOSEPH M. MARTIN (BMI)
and JON PAIGE (BMI)

Hear that glo-ri-ous song in the dis-tance, car-ried on___ the wings of praise. Soon the heav-ens will

shout and pro-claim it. All__ the earth will cel - e - brate.__

Je - sus is com-ing! Je - sus is com-ing! Je - sus is com-ing; pre -

pare the way! Je - sus is com-ing; pre - pare the way!

48

A8530

A8530

Soon the King will come and reign!

Je - sus is com - ing! Je - sus is com - ing!

Je - sus is com - ing; pre - pare the way! Je - sus is com - ing; pre -

NARRATOR:

As the time came for God's promise to unfold, he brought a young girl and a simple carpenter to the tiny village of Bethlehem. In the obscure backdrop of a stable, heaven and earth were joined. The circumstances surrounding this miracle would mystify the logic of many.

Bethlehem Light
O Little Town of Bethlehem

Words by
PHILLIP BROOKS (1831-1893), *alt.*

Arranged by
JOSEPH M. MARTIN (BMI)

* Tune: CLONMEL, Traditional Irish Melody

60

52 **A little quicker, with hushed intensity** (♩ = ca. 88)

How__ si - lent - ly, how si - lent - ly the__ won - drous gift__ is giv'n! So__

* Tune: KINGSFOLD, Traditional English Melody

A8530

62

A8530

* Tune: FOREST GREEN, Traditional English Melody
A8530

hear the Christ - mas an - gels the great glad tid - ings

tell. O come to us, a -

bide with us, our Lord, Em - man - u - el, our

NARRATOR:

Under the cover of night, in the silence of a sleeping town, the Light of the world was born. No royal announcement preceded him; no throngs gathered to welcome him. In a moment of stillness, Light shattered darkness without a sound.

In Silence He Came

Words and Music by
JOSEPH M. MARTIN (BMI)
Incorporating Tune:
STILL, STILL, STILL
Traditional Austrian Carol

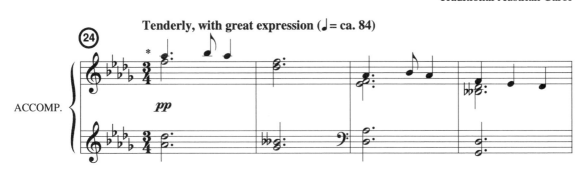

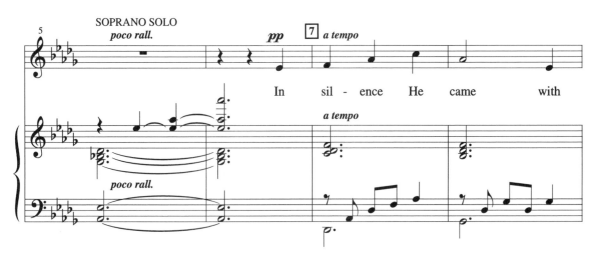

* Tune: STILLE NACHT, Franz Gruber (1787-1863)

A8530

A8530

* Tune: STILL, STILL, STILL; Traditional Austrian Carol

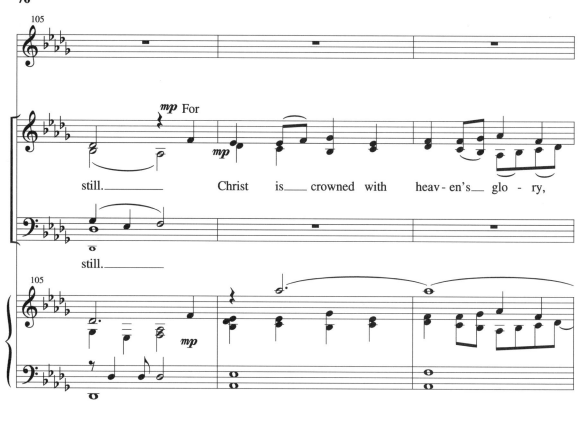

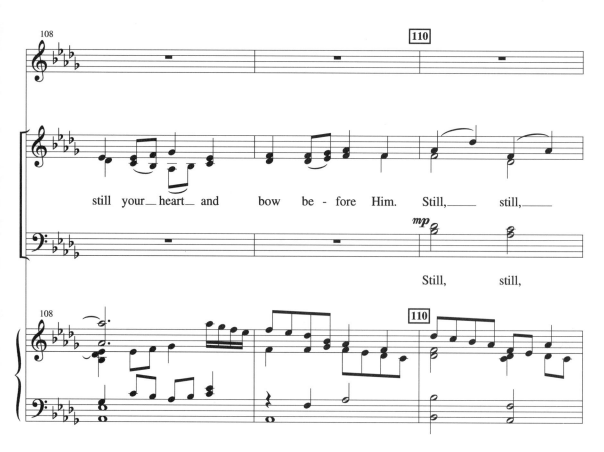

(This page was intentionally left blank.)

NARRATOR:

Shepherds lived in the nearby fields, watching over their flocks. Suddenly, the skies were filled with a blinding light. They were terrified, but an angel of the Lord appeared and gave comfort to them saying, "Be not afraid, for I come to bring you news of great joy! Arise for your Light has come, and he shall be a Savior to all people. You shall find him wrapped in cloths, lying in a manger." When the angel had left them, the shepherds said to one another, "Let us go to Bethlehem to see what has been told to us." When they found the Child, they worshipped him, and quickly spread the news of all they had seen and heard.

Rise and Shine!

Words by
JOSEPH M. MARTIN

Tune: IL EST NÉ
Traditional French Carol
Arranged by
JOSEPH M. MARTIN (BMI)

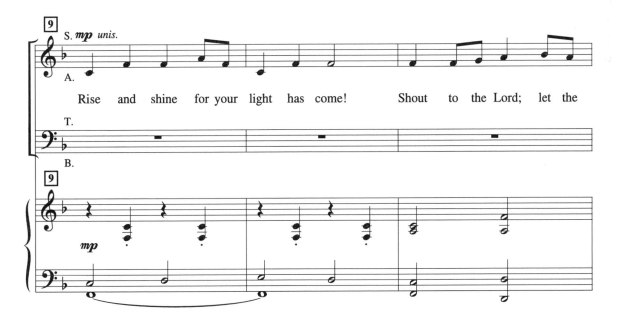

Rise and shine for your light has come! Shout to the Lord; let the

82

A8530

88

* Tune: WERDE MUNTER, Johann Schop (1600-1665)
Words: Martin Janus (1620-1682); trnaslation anonymous, alt.

A8530

A8530

NARRATOR:

A strange new light appeared in the skies, a wondrous star, causing amazement to Magi from the east. This star went ahead of them and they followed it to Bethlehem. When it stopped over the place where the Child was, they were filled with joy, and fell on their knees in worship.

Invitation to the Manger
Oh, Come, Little Children

Words by
CHRISTOPH von SCHMID (1768-1854)
and JOSEPH M. MARTIN

Music by
JOHANN A. SCHULZ (1747-1800)
Arranged by
JOSEPH M. MARTIN (BMI)

A8530

night.

Oh, come to the man - ger, the

Sav - ior is born; come out of the shad - ows and wor - ship the Lord.

Oh,

Underscore

Music by
JOSEPH M. MARTIN (BMI)

NARRATOR: Unto us a Child is born and to us a Son is given. For God, who said, "Let light shine out of darkness," has made his Light shine in our hearts in the face of Christ.

* Music: CRANHAM, Gustav Holst (1874-1934)

A8530

All is Calm, All is Bright
Silent Night, Holy Night

Words by
JOSEPH MOHR (1792-1848)

Tune: STILLE NACHT
by FRANZ GRUBER (1787-1863)
Arranged by
JOSEPH M. MARTIN (BMI)

* Accompaniment is optional through measure 27.

A8530

110

A8530

Christ,____ the Sav - ior, is born!"

Si - lent night, ho - ly night!

116

A8530

NARRATOR:
No one who lights a candle puts it under a basket, but on a stand, that all may see. In the same way, let your light shine that others may see it. For once you were darkness, but now you are light. Go now in peace, and live as children of light.

for Jonathan and Aubrey

A Blessing of Light

Words and Music by
JOSEPH M. MARTIN (BMI)

* If performed with Children's Choir or Solo, S.A.T.B. Choir enters at measure 11.

120

A8530

122

A8530

(This page was intentionally left blank.)

An Advent Credo

FLUTE

Flute Arrangement by
JOSEPH M. MARTIN *and*
BRANT ADAMS